TALK
TO THE
book

JESS CASTLE

Big mouth

PICK A **COLOR** THAT SAYS THE **MOST** ABOUT **YOU.**

DO YOU HAVE A *lucky* **NUMBER?**

ARE YOU **SUPERSTITIOUS?**

....

....

....

....

....

WRITE YOUR **FULL NAME**
IN A STYLE THAT SUITS YOUR
PERSONALITY.

COVER AS MUCH OF THE PAGE AS YOUR **PERSONALITY** WILL ALLOW.

COVER THIS PAGE IN DOODLES THAT DESCRIBE THE WAY YOU ARE **FEELING RIGHT NOW.**

COVER THIS PAGE IN DOODLES THAT DESCRIBE
HOW YOU WOULD *really* LIKE TO FEEL.

CIRCLE THE WORDS THAT BEST DESCRIBE **YOU.**

CONTENT ★ AMBITIOUS

BRAVE ★ CAUTIOUS

PRINCIPLED ★ SENSITIVE

EMOTIONAL ★ *opinionated*

ATTENTIVE ★ CARELESS

STRONG-WILLED

OUTGOING ★ HILARIOUS

OPTIMISTIC ★ **FEARFUL**

IMPETUOUS ★ EARNEST

generous ★ HAPPY

PRACTICAL ★ **SASSY**

FORGETFUL ★ *creative*

SMART ★ **OPEN-MINDED**

NAIVE ★ GREGARIOUS

WRITE SOMETHING ABOUT **YOURSELF** THAT NOBODY ELSE KNOWS, THEN COVER IT IN DOODLES SO **NO ONE** CAN READ IT.

IF YOUR LIFE WAS A **NOVEL,**
WHAT WOULD ITS **TITLE** BE?

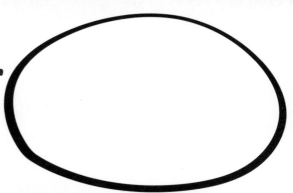

WHO WOULD THE **3** MAIN **CHARACTERS** BE?

1.

2.

3.

WHAT **GENRE**
WOULD IT BE?

ACTION

COMEDY

DRAMA

ROMANCE

WRITE THE **BLURB.**

_____
_____
_____
_____
_____
_____
_____

WHEN IS "TOO MUCH" JUST ENOUGH?

WHEN IS "A LITTLE" MORE THAN PLENTY?

WRITE DOWN **3** THINGS IN YOUR LIFE OVER WHICH YOU HAVE **TOTAL CONTROL**.

WRITE DOWN **3** THINGS IN YOUR LIFE OVER WHICH YOU HAVE **NO CONTROL**.

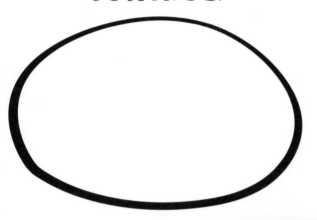

WHAT'S NOT WORTH **WORRYING** ABOUT?

WHAT IS THE
FUNNIEST
THING YOU'VE EVER SEEN?

WHAT IS THE
SADDEST
THING YOU'VE EVER SEEN?

DO YOU BELIEVE IN **FATE?**

WHAT IS **GOOD LUCK?**

....

....

....

....

....

....

WHAT DOES

LOVE

LOOK LIKE?

DRAW IT HERE.

THREE TIMES WHEN YOUR

HEAD

HAS RULED YOUR HEART:

1. _____

_____

2. _____

_____

3. _____

_____

THREE TIMES WHEN YOUR *heart*

HAS RULED YOUR HEAD:

1. _____

_____

_____

2. _____

_____

_____

3. _____

_____

_____

DO YOU EVER **WISH** YOU WEREN'T SO **WELL-BEHAVED?**

 YES! NO!

WHAT'S THE **WORST** THING YOU'VE EVER DONE?

_____
_____
_____
_____
_____
_____
_____
_____
_____
_____

WHAT'S THE **KINDEST** THING YOU'VE **EVER** DONE?

TOUCH

TASTE

SMELL

IF YOU HAD A *secret* TATTOO, WHERE WOULD IT BE?

IF YOU COULD GAIN ONE SUPERPOWER, WHAT WOULD IT BE?

_____

_____

_____

_____

_____

YES OR NO?

DO YOU BELIEVE WORLD PEACE WILL EVER BE POSSIBLE?

YES!   NO!

WILL WE EVER LIVE TO 200 YEARS OLD?

YES!   NO!

IS THERE A LIMIT TO INVENTION?

YES!   NO!

WILL WE EVER LIVE IN SPACE?

YES!   NO!

IF YOU **HAD** TO MAKE THE **CHOICE**, WOULD YOU BE:

TEN YEARS **YOUNGER** OR **TEN YEARS OLDER?**

DO YOU REMEMBER
YOUR DREAMS?

WHAT KEEPS YOU
AWAKE AT NIGHT?

DO YOU HAVE A RECURRING DREAM OR NIGHTMARE?

3 THINGS YOU HOPE ARE TRUE:

3 THINGS YOU KNOW ARE TRUE:

RECORD YOUR *dreams* FOR A WEEK.

MONDAY

TUESDAY

WEDNESDAY

THURSDAY

FRIDAY

SATURDAY

SUNDAY

SUMMARY

THREE CHARACTER TRAITS YOU
ADMIRE
IN OTHER PEOPLE:

1. _____

2. _____

3 _____

THREE CHARACTER TRAITS YOU
DEPLORE
IN OTHER PEOPLE:

1. _____

2. _____

3 _____

YOUR THREE **BEST**
CHARACTERISTICS:

1.

2.

3.

YOUR THREE **WORST** CHARACTERISTICS:

1.

2.

3.

IF YOU COULD BE **MORE** OF SOMETHING, WHAT WOULD IT BE?

IF YOU COULD BE **LESS** OF SOMETHING, WHAT WOULD IT BE?

DOES YOUR NAME SUIT YOUR **PERSONALITY?**

YES! NO!

ARE YOU THE SAME PERSON ON THE **INSIDE** AS YOU ARE ON THE **OUTSIDE?**

YES! NO!

DRAW HOW YOU **FEEL** ON THE INSIDE.

DRAW YOURSELF AS AN EMOJI.

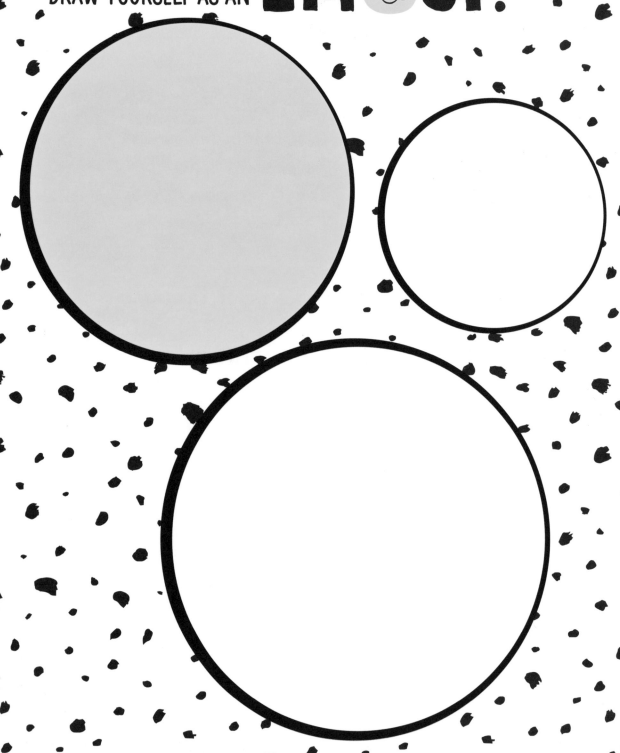

ARE THESE QUALITIES

↑ OVERRATED   **OR**   UNDERRATED? ↓

↑ ↓

HONESTY

INTEGRITY

SELF-DEPRECATION

SELF-CONFIDENCE

MODESTY

RESPECTABILITY

WRITE THE THINGS THAT **MAKE YOU**...

HAPPY

SAD

ANGRY

RATE THE FOLLOWING

OUT OF 10:

ADMIRATION ☐

ADULATION ☐

APPRECIATION ☐

COMRADERY ☐

CERTAINTY ☐

CONSISTENCY ☐

PREDICTABILITY ☐

SECURITY ☐

IF YOU COULD CHOOSE TO **LIVE** FOREVER, WOULD YOU?

_____

_____

_____

_____

_____

_____

_____

YES OR NO?

IS IT EVER OK TO LIE? Y ☐ N ☐

IS IT OK TO LIE TO MAKE SOMEONE FEEL GOOD? Y ☐ N ☐

IS IT OK TO LIE TO SOMEONE IF IT'S FOR THEIR OWN GOOD? Y ☐ N ☐

IS IT EVER OK TO LIE TO GET SOMEONE OUT OF TROUBLE? Y ☐ N ☐

IS IT EVER OK TO LIE TO GET YOURSELF OUT OF TROUBLE? Y ☐ N ☐

YOU ARE ON A CROWDED TRAIN OR BUS:
NAME **3** THINGS THAT **ANNOY** YOU.

1. _____

2. _____

3. _____

NAME **3** THINGS YOU HAVE DONE TO MAKE
SOMEONE'S JOURNEY MORE PLEASANT:

1

3

2

WHERE WOULD YOU **RATHER** BE RIGHT NOW?

WORDS OR PHRASES
YOU USE **TOO OFTEN:**

THINGS YOU
DON'T SAY OFTEN ENOUGH:

THE **5** BEST *compliments*

ANYONE HAS EVER GIVEN YOU:

1 _____

_____

2 _____

_____

3 _____

_____

4 _____

_____

5 _____

_____

WHAT'S YOUR GREATEST
TALENT?

WHAT'S YOUR
PET PEEVE?

WHAT'S YOUR BIGGEST
WEAKNESS?

DO YOU HAVE A SECRET HABIT
THAT **NOBODY**
KNOWS ABOUT?

WHAT DOES **FEAR** LOOK LIKE? DRAW IT HERE.

WHAT'S THE MOST
GENEROUS
THING YOU'VE EVER DONE?

HOW DID IT MAKE YOU FEEL?

WHAT IS THE **FIRST** THING YOU'D DO IF YOU BECAME A **MILLIONAIRE?**

AND THE **SECOND?**

AND THE **THIRD?**

WHO OR WHAT WAS THE **BIGGEST**
INFLUENCE ON YOU AS A CHILD?

IN A **GOOD** WAY?

IN A **BAD** WAY?

IF YOUR LIFE WAS A **MOVIE,**
WHAT WOULD IT BE CALLED?

CAST IT HERE.

_ _ _ _ _ _ _ _ _ _ _ _ _ _ _

_ _ _ _ _ _ _ _ _ _ _ _ _ _ _

_ _ _ _ _ _ _ _ _ _ _ _ _ _ _ WHO WOULD PLAY YOUR **BEST FRIEND?**

_ _ _ _ _ _ _ _ _ _ _ _ _ _ _

_ _ _ _ _ _ _ _ _ _ _ _ _ _ _ WHO WOULD PLAY YOUR **ROMANTIC INTEREST?**

_ _ _ _ _ _ _ _ _ _ _ _ _ _ _

_ _ _ _ _ _ _ _ _ _ _ _ _ _ _ WHO WOULD PLAY **YOU?**

_ _ _ _ _ _ _ _ _ _ _ _ _ _ _ WHO WOULD PLAY THE **VILLAIN?**

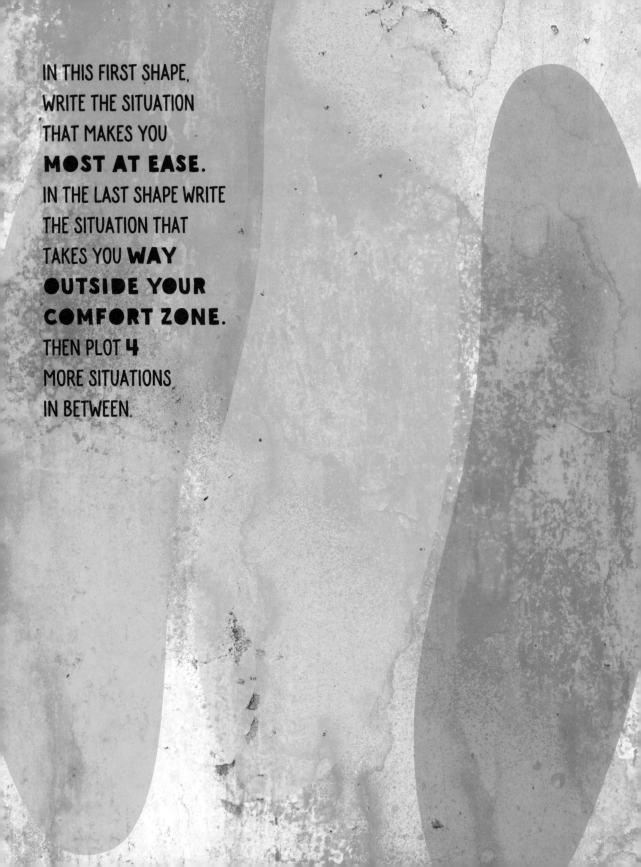

IN THIS FIRST SHAPE,
WRITE THE SITUATION
THAT MAKES YOU
MOST AT EASE.
IN THE LAST SHAPE WRITE
THE SITUATION THAT
TAKES YOU **WAY**
OUTSIDE YOUR
COMFORT ZONE.
THEN PLOT **4**
MORE SITUATIONS
IN BETWEEN.

GIVE UP

FOR A CAUSE YOU BELIEVE IN?

1. ....
....
....

2. ....
....
....

3. ....
....
....

IS IT BETTER TO GIVE **TIME** OR **MONEY** TO SOMETHING YOU **CARE** ABOUT?

WHAT DOES **ANGER** LOOK LIKE? DRAW IT HERE.

WHAT DOES *peace* LOOK LIKE? DRAW IT HERE.

WHO WAS YOUR FIRST **BEST FRIEND?**

WHAT DREW YOU **TOGETHER?**

ARE YOU STILL IN TOUCH WITH THEM?

WHAT KEPT YOU **TOGETHER** OR DREW YOU **APART?**

WRITE THE **STORY** OF HOW YOU MET.

WHO WAS YOUR FIRST **BOYFRIEND** OR **GIRLFRIEND?**

WHAT DREW YOU **TOGETHER?**

_____

_____

_____

_____

_____

ARE YOU STILL IN TOUCH WITH THEM? **YES!** **NO!**

WHAT KEPT YOU **TOGETHER...**

OR DREW YOU **APART?**

WRITE THE STORY OF YOUR *first date.*

RANK **5** FRIENDS IN ORDER OF WHO MOST REMINDS YOU OF YOUR **MOTHER.**

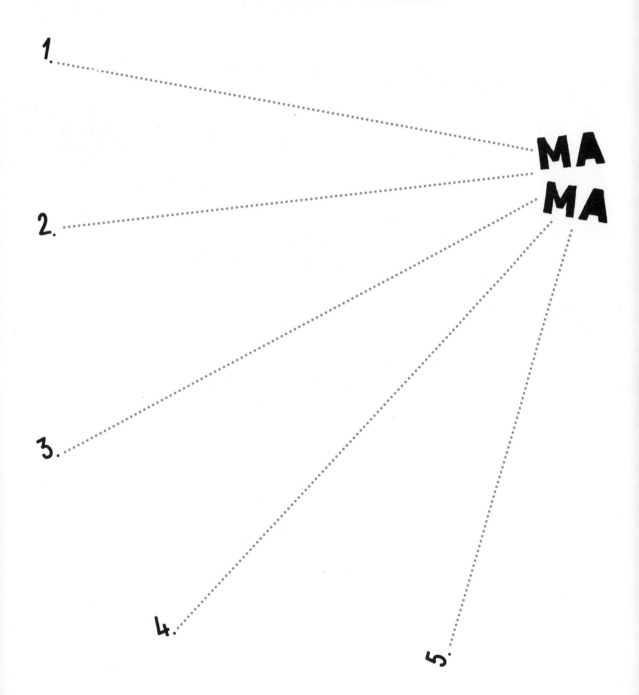

1.

2.

3.

4.

5.

MA MA

HOW MANY **FRIENDS** CAN YOU BE
A **GOOD** FRIEND TO?

IF YOU COULD KEEP **ONE** FRIEND **FOREVER,**
WHO WOULD IT BE?

WOULD YOU GIVE UP **SOCIAL MEDIA**
FOR A TRUE FRIEND FOR **LIFE?**

1.

2.

3.

4.

LIST **FOUR**
FRIENDS IN ORDER
OF WHO IS MOST
LIKE **YOU.**

IF YOU COULD HAVE A **PET** FOR LIFE OR A **FRIEND** FOR LIFE, WHICH WOULD YOU CHOOSE? ....

HAVE YOU EVER STRUCK UP A CONVERSATION WITH A **STRANGER?**

 YES!

☐ NO!

WHAT'S **BETTER:**

MEETING **OLD** FRIENDS

OR

MAKING **NEW** FRIENDS?

WHAT **DID YOU** (OR WOULD YOU) **TALK** ABOUT?

_____

_____

_____

_____

WHAT MAKES YOU MORE
COMFORTABLE:

CERTAINTY OR **UNCERTAINTY?**

KNOWLEDGE OR **IGNORANCE?**

ENDLESS OPPORTUNITY OR **LIMITED CHOICE?**

THE JOURNEY OR **THE ARRIVAL?**

WHAT ARE YOUR TOP **3** FEARS?

1

2

3

CAN YOU HAVE TOO MUCH OF A **GOOD** THING?

IS THERE A LIMIT TO **PROGRESS?**

IS THERE ANYTHING YOU CAN'T **FORGIVE?**

HOW **FREE** SHOULD **SPEECH** BE?

IS YOUR **BUSINESS** ANYONE ELSE'S?

DO YOU HAVE THE RIGHT TO **JUDGE?**

WHAT IS **MORE** IMPORTANT:

WEALTH OR **KNOWLEDGE?**

HEALTH OR **HAPPINESS?**

PRIVACY OR **SECURITY?**

IF YOU HAD TO SPEND THE REST OF YOUR **LIFE** IN **ONE PLACE**, WHERE WOULD YOU CHOOSE?

WHO WOULD YOU BE WITH?

WHAT ARE **3** THINGS YOU CAN'T LIVE WITHOUT?

1   **2**   **3**

WHAT WOULD YOUR *dream home* LOOK LIKE?

WHO'S THE **WISEST** PERSON YOU'VE EVER MET?

WHAT DO YOU HAVE IN **COMMON?**

HOW DOES THIS PERSON **INSPIRE** YOU?

DO YOU EVER **WISH** YOU'D LISTENED
TO YOUR **TEACHERS** MORE?

YES!   NO!

NAME **3** TEACHERS YOU REMEMBER AND WHY.
USE **5** WORDS OR FEWER FOR EACH.

1   **2**   **3**

_____ _____ _____

_____ _____ _____

_____ _____ _____

_____ _____ _____

_____ _____ _____

WHAT WERE YOUR FAVORITE **CLASSES** AT SCHOOL?

– – – – – – – – – – – – – – –

DESCRIBE YOUR **PROUDEST** SCHOOL MOMENT.

DESCRIBE YOUR MOST **MORTIFYING** SCHOOL MOMENT.

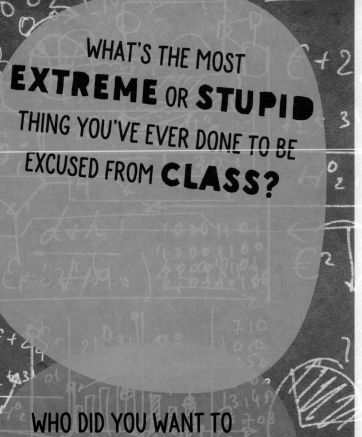

WHAT'S THE MOST **EXTREME** OR **STUPID** THING YOU'VE EVER DONE TO BE EXCUSED FROM **CLASS?**

WHO DID YOU WANT TO **IMPRESS** MORE:

TEACHERS

OR

FRIENDS?

LIST THE AWARDS YOU'VE **WON:**

LIST THE AWARDS YOU **WISH** YOU'D WON:

LIST THE **COUNTRIES** ON YOUR

TRAVEL

bucket list:

....

....

....

....

....

PICK **2** COMPANIONS FOR A TOUR AROUND THE **WORLD**.

....

WHAT **3** THINGS WOULD YOU ....

HAVE TO TAKE WITH YOU? ....

....

YOU ARE IN THE MIDDLE SEAT ON A **PLANE;**
WHO'S EITHER SIDE OF **YOU?**

BEST CASE:

WORST CASE:

1. ....

1. ....

2. ....

2. ....

THE **BEST** THING ABOUT FLYING:

....

THE **WORST** THING ABOUT FLYING:

....

WOULD YOU JOIN A
SPACE MISSION?

YES! ☐   ☐ NO!

IS EARNING WEALTH MORALLY SUPERIOR TO *winning* IT? WHY?

_____

_____

_____

_____

_____

_____

_____

IS WINNING WEALTH MORALLY SUPERIOR TO *inheriting* IT? WHY?

_____

_____

_____

_____

_____

_____

_____

_____

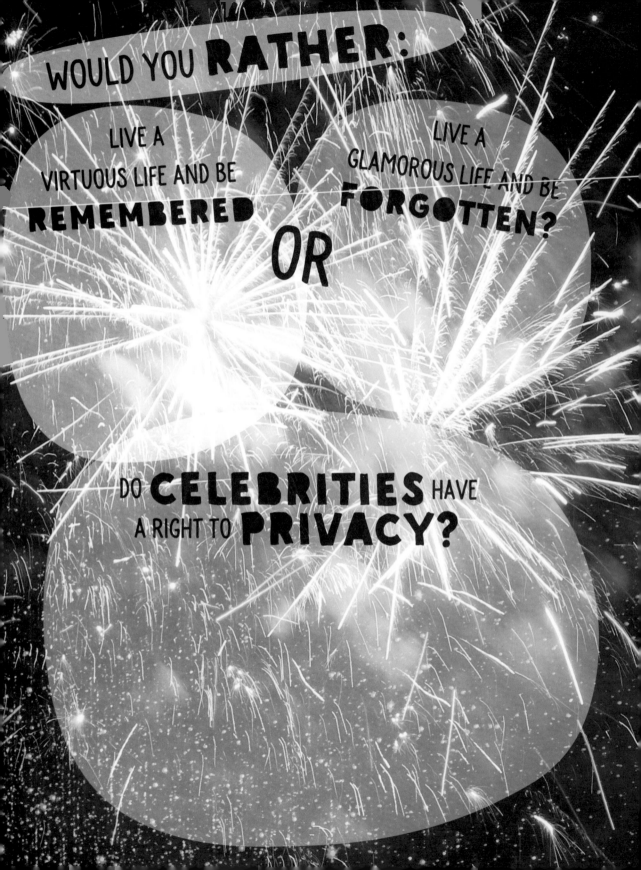

WOULD YOU **RATHER:**

LIVE A VIRTUOUS LIFE AND BE **REMEMBERED**

OR

LIVE A GLAMOROUS LIFE AND BE **FORGOTTEN?**

DO **CELEBRITIES** HAVE A RIGHT TO **PRIVACY?**

5 LAWS YOU WOULD MAKE:

1.

2.

3.

4.

5.

FIVE LAWS
YOU WOULD REPEAL:

1. _____

_____

2. _____

_____

3. _____

_____

4 _____

_____

5. _____

_____

WOULD YOU **RATHER:**

BE **FITTER** OR BE **SMARTER?**

WHY?

....

....

BE AN **ONLY CHILD** OR   HAVE **10 SIBLINGS?**

WHY?

....

....

BE **BETTER LOOKING** OR BE **MORE RESPECTED?**

WHY?

....

....

LOSE YOUR SENSE
OF **STYLE**
OR
YOUR SENSE OF
HUMOR?

WHY?
....
....

BE A RESPECTED
SCHOLAR
OR BE A FAMOUS **ARTIST?**
WHY?
....
....

BE CELEBRATED FOR
YOUR **ACTIONS**
OR FOR YOUR **IDEAS?**
WHY?
....
....

BE HAPPY IN A
TRAILER

OR

BE MISERABLE IN A
PALACE?

WHY?

....

....

....

....

BE FAMOUS FOR
GIVING

OR

BE FAMOUS FOR
WINNING?

WHY?

....

....

....

HAVE FAMOUS
PARENTS

OR

HAVE FAMOUS
SIBLINGS?

WHY?

....

....

....

HAVE **NO PHONE**

OR

HAVE **NO SHOES?**

WHY?

....

....

....

....

OWN AN **ANTIQUE PAINTING**

OR

OWN A **VINTAGE CAR?**

WHY?

....

....

....

....

SPEND YOUR LIFE **ABROAD**

OR

NEVER LEAVE YOUR **HOME TOWN?**

WHY?

....

....

....

NAME SOMETHING YOU WANT TO **ACHIEVE** IN...

THE NEXT **5** YEARS:

THE NEXT **10** YEARS:

THE NEXT **20** YEARS:

FILL THIS PAGE WITH THINGS YOU WANT TO *achieve* IN YOUR **LIFETIME.**

WHAT DOES THE **FUTURE** LOOK LIKE?
DRAW IT HERE.

WHAT ARE THE FIVE BEST THINGS YOUR
future
COULD HOLD?

_____

_____

_____

_____

_____

_____

_____

_____

_____

WRITE A LETTER TO **YOURSELF** AS A *caring* FRIEND.

_____

_____

_____

_____

_____

_____

_____

_____

_____